Sustainable and affordable housing

SOCIAL HOUSING BARCELONA

Francesco Cocco - Massimo Faiferri

Photos by Stefano Ferrando

INDEX

	Massimo Faiferri
4	**The urban dimension of contemporary architecture**

	Francesco Cocco
22	**The communal space project in collective housing**

	Francesco Cocco
30	**Active aging in the model of *viviendas dotacionales***

28-29	**PROJECTS**
40	**1** REINA AMALIA *Eduard Bru i Buster, Neus la Comba Mongé, Victor Setoian Perego*
48	**2** SANTA CATERINA *EMBT Arquitectes Associats*
56	**3** CIBELES *EXE Arquitectura*
64	**4** TORRE JULIA *Paul Vidal, Sergi Pons, Ricard Galiana*
72	**5** CAN TRAVI *Sergi Serrat*
80	**6** PASSEIG URRUTIA *Joan Callís, Pia Wortham*
88	**7** NAVAS DE TOLOSA *Nogué Onzain López Arquitectes*
96	**8** RODALIES *Conxita Balcells associats*
104	**9** GLORIES *Esteve Bonell, Josep M. Gil, Marta Peris, José Toral*
112	**10** CAMÍ ANTIC DE VALENCIA *Sara Bartomeus, Anna Renau*

	Josep Maria Montaner
120	**Public housing: the Barcelona model**

Massimo Faiferri

The urban dimension
of contemporary architecture

City and residence

The issue of *inhabiting* seems to have long lost the central role it had in terms of legislation and regulatory guidelines in the pioneering phase of the Twentieth century. In fact, the issue of housing has played a central role in European urban and architectural culture since the very beginning and in particular since the 1950s. During the last decades of the Twentieth century, however, it lost importance to the point that much research focused almost entirely on building and production aspects, which are usually separated from the urban, residential and innovative characteristics of housing solutions. After losing this standardized approach, (private and public) residential construction produced poor urban and territorial housing solutions, lacking not only a structural project but also a political and social one. This has resulted in fragments of city that are shapeless and devoid of urbanity, as can easily be perceived in most European suburbs, and in preventing the term *inhabit,* meaning an integrated human and social experience, from reflecting society, i.e. from depicting the way people experience their home and context, as an element revealing more general socio-cultural and political trends.

Most contemporary suburbs consist of a mix of undifferentiated elements, where accessibility is the only unifying factor and public spaces and services no longer have a structuring role, but simply become a matter of quantity. The growth of European cities has frequently been handled favoring quantitative and economic aspects, rather than qualitative ones. The search for an effective way to create an ideal urban community, shared by citizens and their institutions, has come to a halt as there is no ideal model of a city to which to aspire or compete with. The variety of opinions on the city expressed by different disciplines, often contradictory, have not merged to establish a common objective. Instead, a specialized vision of the urban phenomenon has been maintained, resulting in the loss of the one and only goal of planning: architecture, the city and their reciprocal relationship.

Cibeles

Nevertheless, if the city is still considered the primary place for social life, and architecture should create the best conditions for social life to progress, research and experiments favoring the urban dimension of architecture need to be intensified. This idea is deeply rooted in European architectural culture, in which at least two possible ways of development can be identified. The first concerns the construction of sizeable urban settlements and aims at creating urban segments within a relatively short timeframe, compared with the lengthy construction times of the city based on development and transformation projects trying to integrate the specific features of the various stakeholders involved in the process. The effort to coordinate the construction, infrastructure and landscape components, aiming at a community appearance and complexity of uses able to motivate innovation and transformation processes for vast urban areas, stands out as an organized practice attempting to resist the inevitable sequence of changes in shape, plan and policies that accompany these processes. In doing so, it proves to be one of the few approaches that can shape large, complex portions of cities, outline new forms, and propose innovative lifestyles and new uses, avoiding the risk of building uniform districts in terms of functionality and volume. By reconnecting with, reviewing and renewing the Nineteenth century tradition of studies on the European city, this approach attempts to give shape to an inclusive, pluralist city, able to accommodate changes in use and transformation over a sufficiently extensive timespan as to contribute to settlement phenomena.

Whereas the process of starting up, monitoring and managing this kind of urban project is a long one involving many steps, urban architecture design has more limited goals. The second approach to the development of the urban dimension of design is actually connected with interpreting the single architectural project. From this point of view, a set of projects can be referred to that share a common background, a European one in particular, labeled "urban project" by Ignasi De Solà-Morales. Since the 1970s many architects have tried to enliven parts of cities, starting up a tradition where architectural works seem to look for each other within urban spaces. In these cases, architecture takes the city itself, its remains, memories and fragments as sources of inspiration, sometimes as constraints, sometimes as opportunities for design, linking up with the urban history and buildings of the past, and initiating interplay that can help to innovate the life of the city and its inhabitants. This leads to the reinterpretation of an existing place, which is enhanced while respecting tradition and innovation. Such a perspective, which aims at maintaining and reorganizing, articulating and integrating new and existing solutions, tradition with innovation, shows the importance still today of the idea of creating an urban fabric linking past, present and future. Hence, the idea takes shape of design that aims at superseding the unproductive separation of town planning and architectural project thanks to the introduction of the concept of "intermediate scale", intended as a way to check and mediate programmatic and structural decisions. In this way distance is taken from some of the studies on the European city of the past that led to conservative approaches, opening up instead to the urban transformation potential typical of contemporary metropolises. The ideal relationship between *architecture* and *city* is covered – again as conceived by De Solà-Morales - by the concept of "territory": a "system of spaces to inhabit, with its own topographic, historical and social identity, a starting and meeting point for the training work inherent in *architecture* and *city*, in whatever sense these terms are intended". In terms of territory, however, what proposals are coming from contemporary architecture and cities? The urban potential of contemporary metropolises, derived from the progressive incorporation of new, unknown aspects of the city, may be the critical element in stimulating a richer and more appropriate process - one with a complex, multilayered history yet able to combine the different aspects of architectural design.

In this sense, it is vital to understand the signs (including political ones) of the rediscovered awareness that urban environments can closely relate to housing still today. The housing policy should no longer be a sole prerogative of the laws regarding the market and profit as it has been over the last few decades. The public housing issue can become an extraordinary opportunity for governments to control and transform the territory, promoting the regeneration of degraded areas and redevelopment of depressed and abandoned areas. The shortage of available building areas, together with the particular fragility of some urban contexts, but also the need to recover huge segments of consolidated urban fabric, are both a problem and an opportunity that European cities must face; especially in terms of the housing issue seen in the light of the social phenomena of immigration, changes in terms of family units and the energy and environmental sustainability essential for any intervention. Therefore, it is necessary to develop both strategies and instruments for analysis and intervention that are suitable for the complexity of contemporary urban phenomena. This means creating new transformation ideas bearing a different concept of density. Contemporary housing design should aim not be an isolated event, but a proponent of new relationships with the landscape and buildings, the road network and other infrastructure, and the public and commercial spaces of the city. The people, their needs and their community forms lie at the heart of the problem, especially in terms of their relationship with the environment. This is one of the few ways design could establish a renewed, productive relationship with city construction.

Hence, the new "relationship of proximity" in housing solutions should be analyzed following the new social trends, overcoming the physical limits of a district so that social relationships can develop their full potential in terms of a new kind of proximity, shaped by the links and connections also provided by technology. In other words, urban architectural design should focus on the relationship between the *house* and the *city*, going beyond the usual disciplinary and operative boundaries. The same approach should also be developed in projects for single buildings, experimenting with a progressive, inevitable hybridization of topics, functions, uses, shapes and materials in order to find the right relationship between the elements of the city and the landscape.

Torre Julia

Barcelona Social Housing

Designing a project within a frame where the new urban phenomena appear so complex and indistinct is undoubtedly a difficult task which presents obvious risks of simplification at an operational level. At the same time, it is a fascinating challenge that should be tackled transversally compared with the established methods, if reference is made to those cases that tried in the past to change, albeit partially, the traditional approaches to planning and the development and completion of cities.

Over the past few decades a number of experiments in several European countries have tried to design a housing project with a new, meaningful relationship between architecture and city. The process produced significant results in a few fortunate places only, one of which was Barcelona, a case that deserves an analytical study.

With the reform of local autonomies that took place after Francisco Franco's death in 1975, local Spanish governments had the chance to directly promote and manage urban regeneration processes, aimed mainly at building public spaces in those portions of the city adversely affected by the great urban expansion of the time. In Barcelona the *Plan General Metropolitano*, approved in 1976, showed itself to be an innovative, efficient urban tool for recovering existing spaces, creating places for community activities, enhancing infrastructure and improving the relationship between city center and suburbs. It selected a few areas of the city that needed prompt intervention, improving public space as a means of urban regeneration. This policy was carried out under the auspices of strict public control, bearing mind the goal of fulfilling collective needs, first and foremost the reappropriation of degraded and abandoned urban areas which were turned into centers for renewed social activities and interactions. Projects were designed in order to give a "domestic" and "social" touch to open spaces: architectural elements decorating the city and green areas played an important role in redeveloping and reinterpreting places in a particularly democratic way, by seeking the principles at the heart of the housing project in the public dimension, too. To a certain extent it can be stated that the relationship between housing and public spaces has been the central topic for town planning and architectural projects in the city of Barcelona since the democratic revival began, and has continued to be developed, following different interpretations, in projects for subsequent decades. This tendency can be seen in the urban changes linked with the 1992 Olympic Games, which marked the transition from an urban dimension to a metropolitan one, but also in the organization of Forum 2004, a cultural event that the municipality of Barcelona used as a chance for a new phase of great works redeveloping and uniting a portion of the city with a huge territorial dimension. It was indeed the Forum experience that seemed, according to Josep Acebillo, to reveal the difficulties of imagining a city based on the "critical urban pragmatism" resulting from the relationship between tower buildings and open spaces. The Forum model shows its limits as it basically failed to establish the close relationship with its surroundings and with the social dimension of inhabiting that previous experiences had shown. On the one hand, the Forum experience represented a crucial chance to redirect urban transformation strategies following a different perspective compared with the preceding years; on the other, it upset the balance between public and private interventions, with the latter now being considerably more important in the decision-making process for city interventions. Over recent decades, the significant growth of private enterprise in many urban transformation projects has resulted in some cases in a reduction in building areas for social housing or assisted private housing, and in the rehabilitation of land and buildings to be used for services, equipment or infrastructure.

This book aims to be more than a simple collection of the urban-architectural transformations that have characterized public housing in the city of Barcelona. In fact, an attempt has been made to analyze and investigate a political-administrative issue that has encouraged multi-faceted development, capable of outlining a trajectory along which architecture, city and housing are evenly balanced within a design experience decisive for urban transformation schemes.

The success of this innovative, administrative and planning work can be attributed to many reasons, including town planning operations, the demand for new housing solutions and the creation of complex urban transformation schemes. One of the most interesting outcomes of this detailed experience concerns the relationship between public and private space.

Between privacy and collectivity

In contemporary design relations between "inside" and "outside" the home, namely domestic privacy and external collectivity, have expanded and branched out to areas able to increase the inhabitant's sense of belonging, possession and expression.

Personal privacy is no longer the exclusive prerogative of the domestic space where, once over the threshold, an inhabitant progressively casts off the social and cultural aids that have ensured them a continuous relationship with the world, to achieve extreme subjectivity, complete solitude and individuality that cannot be shared. Contemporary

Santa Caterina

forms of inhabiting involve a high degree of mingling between domestic and collective, through a system of relations that is more complex than the simple inside/outside pattern. "Going away" does not mean interrupting the experience of inhabiting but renewing it somewhere else, in other ways and with other individuals. The inhabiting experience becomes animated – it is movement tending towards plunging and penetrating, to leave the space inhabited via a series of gestures and rituals that are increasingly automatic, that reproduce the rhythm of a constant dialectic between the inside and outside of the private home nucleus. "Feeling at home" entails continuous entering and leaving, in rhythmic alternation that sketches out our subjective presence in the world. What defines it is a ritual path alternating between exteriority (focused on collective aspects and relations with others) and interiority (which is, ultimately, individual solitude and personal subjectivity).

In the history of western cities the settlement pattern particularly successful in establishing a relationship between the growth processes of the urban dimension and inhabiting was the large *block*, which offered forms able to restore the rituals involving privacy and collectivity often denied by urban dynamics that tended to lead to isolation and exclusion processes of entire segments of the city. Here a wider concept of *home* is referred to, beyond the physical perimeter of the dwelling, encompassing spaces that transcend the private, personal dimension of the house, in a different dimension which acknowledges the place inhabited within the urban system and landscape to which it belongs.

Based on this experience, in order to engage with current dynamics, the landscape of the dwelling has to recompose itself starting with the "in"/"out" ritual within the personal perimeter of the dwelling, concentrating on the quality of the views, their identity and the variety of relations with the whole city, seeking a relationship with both old and new segments and the environmental context. This way the contemporary city can try to reconstruct a continuity of form as in the old city, establishing new relationships between its parts, so as to avoid any isolation.

The projects presented in this anthology build up a mutual relationship in various ways. An initial approach aims to construct an intermediate scale, namely a series of spaces between the public spaces of the city and the private ones of a building. In some cases this "intermediate space" is obtained within the architectural work, such as, for example, the **Reina Amalia** housing complex in the Raval district, where the large openings giving variety to the main façade indicate the presence of a senior day center and a civic center on the ground floor, conceived as spaces of social cohesion in a multiethnic district. When looking at the façade and section of the building it is possible to glimpse the different activities that take place inside. The spaces are divided so as to create a U-system, with a series of intermediate spaces that gradually accompany the visitor from the public space of Folch i Torres Square to the semi-public space of the day center and civic center, through the semi-private space of the inner court, intended as an open space for the inhabitants, to end with the personal, private space of the housing. A similar principle can be found in the **Cibeles** vivienda dotacional project. This takes its name from a dancehall that was previously located there, in the Gracia district, and consists of two separate parts, designed as a primary healthcare center on the lower floors, with the homes for the elderly on the upper floors. Here, too, the public space of the road continues inside the healthcare center through an interconnected section. Even if the space is small, the idea of defining a sequence of intermediate spaces is clear, thanks to vertical distribution on the façade, consisting of a series of ramps linking the public space outside the building with the semi-public internal space. On the upper floors intended for the housing there is also an interesting central space, which succeeds in bringing natural light to all levels of the building. The design of the distribution corridors serving the houses divides the section into spaces with double or triple height, in which the common spaces are situated.

The interior of the building also serves as a semi-public, interconnected, bright space in between the private space of the houses and the public external space. The idea that the distributing element can be used as an extension of the public road and can become a social space for the inhabitants is the core principle of the Torre Julia project. Being one of the symbols of post-Olympic Barcelona, the tower stages a series of semi-public spaces, featuring wide corridors with views of the city, external stairs, double height spaces, multipurpose spaces and terraces designed for community activities. In this building the metropolitan landscape perceived from the different levels contributes to defining the intermediate spaces, reinforcing the idea of a public space that enters the building developing vertically throughout the different floors of the tower. This device helps make the distribution elements of the building more dynamic and introduces the idea of an "ambulatory space" to be experienced through the senses and movement. The large openings in the facades guide the glance outwards and, at the same time, incorporate the landscape in the common spaces, further enriching the users' perceptive experience.

The **Cami antic de Valencia** building also develops the idea of a public space at different levels of the building, through a series of walkways and common spaces that connect the five residential blocks. The gallery model extends the familiar space of the house towards a distributive space that overlooks the two internal patios. One

of these has a more urban nature and is delimited on the ground floor by the civic center open to the district and overlooked by the housing for young people, while the other, accessible from the road, is an urban vegetable garden for the elderly. The private space of the house is gradually permeated by these two elements linking with the public space of the city, so that the user is gradually accompanied from inside his house to the galleries, then through the distributive spaces to the inner patios that are connected to the city. Bearing in mind the idea of inhabiting not being a purely domestic phenomenon, the complex relationship between familiarity and collectivity is assisted by the design of the external spaces. This is also developed on the grounds of its "relational function" with the surrounding urban components: places for services and equipment that turn housing design into the wider one of *inhabiting*. For a project to be defined as urban, the degree of multifunctionality of its dimensional space acquires an important role in the outline and detail of the proposal. In this sense, the *vivienda dotacional* in **Glories**, which offers services for the elderly, is presented as a residential housing program with three different uses. The project includes accommodation for a hundred elderly people, in three separate buildings placed on a double-level base, with a healthcare center and community center for public purposes. This mixed use supports the social network of the district and the communal spaces strengthen the relationship between the community and the district. The base for these services is built according to the Eixample grid, while the dimensions of the houses are designed taking into account the neighboring blocks. The result is an architectural work that communicates with the geometry of the adjacent buildings creating an urban segment with its own specific features.

The same attention to the details of the site can be found in the **Passeig Urrutia** residential complex project. Located in the northern suburbs of Barcelona, on the edge of the Nou Barris urban park, this was built taking into consideration the specific orography of the land and consequently creates a peculiar urban landscape connecting the complex to the adjacent green area. The shape of the new building is consistent with that of a previously existing building and is irregular and uneven; thanks also to attentive positioning of the openings of the houses, it creates both visual and physical contact with the nearby park. The distributive corridor inside the building maintains this irregular tendency, by opening, closing and following the shape of the building, eventually leading into balconies and gathering spaces. Here also, the distribution space is a key element in connecting the different housing units, which are positioned so as to guarantee the best views of the park.

Three other projects try to recreate this relationship by offering public space within

Santa Caterina

the complex able to become the core around which the buildings are arranged, by designing the edges of the area in relation to the immediate surroundings and delimiting the open space in the middle. The **Rodalies** project takes shape as a significant building spread out around a large central patio. The northern, southern and eastern façades follow the perimeter of the block, while the western façade curves adapting to the urban scheme of the old district of Barceloneta opposite. In contrast, the **Navas de Tolosa** building is organized in two separated blocks which overlook a symbolic point of the district: the corner formed by the two main roads. The corner solution, typical of the Eixample block by Ildefons Cerdà, is dematerialized creating a viewing cone over the internal square. Social activities for the elderly take place in the two community halls on the ground floor, the large terrace on the third floor and in the pleasant urban garden in the loft. The geometry of the **Can Travi** building is simple, with its large base containing all the district services open to the city. It is delimited by two rows of apartments that determine a domestic, familiar dimension of inhabiting and mediate its relationship with the surroundings through an attentive definition of the perimeter. The strong features of the façades (resulting from the choice to position the terrace within the walls of the building so as to not protrude externally) increase the dimension of the housing units and contribute to the creation of an inhabited landscape, trying to offer different ways of establishing a relationship between inside and outside.

New urban policies

The analysis of these experiments highlights the extraordinary opportunity offered by architectural planning - of housing in particular - to define new urban landscapes that take into account the irreversible transformation processes arising from the changing patterns in contemporary living. In many European cities the younger age group tends more and more frequently to move from the old centers to the suburbs, while a process of depopulation and demographic ageing tends to be almost irremediable in smaller towns. The elderly often have to adapt to emergency solutions, moving in with their children or into private residences in order to be granted the necessary assistance. Consequently, specific policies should be adopted for these categories that will envisage economically accessible housing solutions. The *vivienda dotacional* experiment in Barcelona city is a significant example of how to face these new social emergencies by diversifying types of production and building conventional housing together with specific housing solutions for the young and the elderly. The projects presented in this book feature compact dwellings, with communal spaces and services for the district, characterized by accessible rents and contracts for up to a maximum of 5 years, in order to guarantee equal turns for those granted housing. The success of this housing model lies in its positive effects in terms of urban planning, with the inclusion of services for the district inside the residential buildings, but also, from the social perspective, in housing that attracts inhabitants, stimulating community life and preserving social cohesion. These projects favor and support relations between the inside and outside of the building, i.e. physical and visual links between dwelling and public space that are able to create new collective spaces or host others within that are designed for a variety of activities in addition to the residential function. The housing issue requires a plan capable of ensuring a wide range of different dimensions and types, so as to grant the single users differentiated solutions adapted to the changes in individual requirements and behavior over time. The Barcelona experiment recommends, on the one hand, integrated housing materials which take into account the specific morphological and environmental conditions and, on the other, a high degree of flexibility in terms of spaces, through wise use of "fixed points" and "changing scopes" offered to the single users for the completion and appropriation of houses. This experiment serves as a reminder, moreover, of the vital importance of having outside living spaces (a veranda, a terrace, appropriate roofing, a green area, however small) especially in some Mediterranean regions. It also emphasizes the importance of integrating models, both in terms of sustainability and of social well-being or vitality, in the conscious search to improve the difficult relationship between the individual and the community. Finally, it recalls that today the quality of inhabiting does not depend solely on the quality of single dwellings, but on the quality of the urban environment in which they are located, which lies in the variety of places that contemporary housing design is still capable of generating.

Navas de Tolosa

Francesco Cocco

The communal space project in collective housing

The failure in the urban planning of large functional areas and the decreasing necessity to expand the centers in contemporary cities led to the idea of completing the city through small-scale actions, often with collective housing solutions which regenerate the urban system. If few years ago the city seemed destined to decline creating a suburban future, today it regained importance in the western housing culture and it proves to be a fruitful ground for the experimentation of new housing models capable of meeting the changed needs of the inhabitants of contemporary cities. Collective housing is facing the challenge of creating quality spaces that generate a complex social life compared with the non-qualitative uniformity of the suburban territory. The contemporary house needs to prove to be flexible in terms of private spaces in order to adapt to different lifestyles. However, its chances of succeeding depend on the functional, symbolic and visual relationship between the accommodation, the building and the city. Those city segments that are still partially designed and devoid of the typical activities of a consolidated city, are granted an urban feeling thanks to the presence of a public space and several non-residential functions. Therefore, creating an individual and quiet space is not enough. The house needs to be not only a physical protection but also a tool for a person to build their microcosm. Social well-being and communication are vital in order to avoid that the needs of our time, in terms of privacy and individuality, lead to the isolation of the inhabitants of the city. The accommodation has to overcome the boundaries of the private sphere and to be prepared for unexpected meetings, to influence and to be influenced, and has to extend to the surrounding environment, the district and the city. Collective housing is to be considered more as a territorial infrastructure than as a limited element within the urban system. As in the past, the collective housing model opens itself towards the city in order to share spaces and services. The brand new housing culture sees the accommodation opening itself towards shared, semi-private and public spaces that host activities designed for the neighbors and the inhabitants in order to provide the community with meeting and socialization places. Public space recovers its importance as a cohesive force capable of overcoming the separation between public and private scopes that are considered together. The boundaries disappear or become unstable, and public spaces enter the new collective housing complex as a structuring element of the project. Public space, which varies from the more private model of the American gated communities to the more open and participative solutions hosting several activities during the daytime, becomes an intermediate between the urban and the architectural project by encouraging people to meet in a place that they share. It is a shared space more than a public one, and it overcomes its urbanistic and political ideas. This way, hybrid spaces are created which are more similar to squares and streets than to patios and corridors. The communal space multiplies within the building itself, reversing, in its applications, the way of thinking about residential spaces: the building as a collective space where to create private ones. As a consequence, the communal space is to be found not only outside the building. In this sense, the communicating horizontal elements become potential social spaces, the façades lose their continuity leaving generous open spaces that host shared places. Public space is taking over. The formal definition of the different degrees of privacy, the rational and clear management of the entrances, the relationship between open and built spaces are some of the key themes of the contemporary urban residence project, whether it be a new construction or a recovery of the existing one. Therefore, inter-residential spaces are needed in order to protect the personal sphere while at the same time opening it up towards the community for social purposes. The creation of a public space in the collective housing project requires intermediate elements between public and private, open and closed, collective and individual scopes, which are commonly defined in architectural studies as transition spaces. These are planning tools capable of

Passeig Urrutia

uniting the city and the housing model by supporting the mixture of public and private elements. If transition spaces were almost non-existent until the 19th century, with the exception of a few cases such as the Rue Rivoli in Paris, then it was during the 20th century when the European territory started to produce many examples of residential buildings featuring a relationship between public and private spheres in a wide range of variations. Communal areas like entrances, halls, stairs and corridors are designed as generous spaces that not only allow the residents to access their household units, but work perfectly as a filter between public and private creating a community feeling among the inhabitants of the building. If connected to other portions of the complex, such as terraces, roofing, courts and patios, these spaces can gain an identity and become social spaces. Galleries can become charming porticoes providing a broader space opposite the accommodations. Transition spaces have a communal and public vocation, and thus they guarantee a pleasant walk through different degrees of intimacy and fulfill unexpected purposes. These spaces can be presented in the three different scales of the project, where they can fulfill several roles according to the scope that is considered. As a consequence, spaces with a bigger public vocation are created in order to establish the necessary relationship between the building and the city. Intermediate and communal transition spaces can address the lack of habitable space within households with different uses, while private transition spaces guarantee some flexibility in the more private sphere. It is necessary to end mono-functional projects and extend the functional practices in terms of places and timing in order to guarantee a vital and secure public space. Having multifunctional uses results in a constant presence of people throughout the day which increases security, upholds a good level of maintenance and vitality of the spaces, and thus reduces the common critical issues of the inner city. Multifunctionality becomes the goal of the project: presenting services for the community generates activities that are not only residential, and attracts citizens from outside the district. The development of a sense of identity and belonging to the place in which one lives is one of the most critical elements to be encouraged so that tenants move from being mere beneficiaries of a service to active participants in strengthening their surroundings. When approaching a housing project, different degrees of flexibility are needed, meaning that the public space has to adapt and contribute to different configurations. It is vital to shape a flexible boundary between public and private in order to promote spaces with different uses where to build social and cultural bonds. The household project needs to be part of a complex and pluralistic urban project, where buildings support communal networks and social partners. Therefore, it is crucial to imagine living spaces as "residential infrastructures" capable of "making a city": buildings that fulfill different purposes from the usual residential ones, through the creation of spaces that support sharing and supportive processes.

Torre Julia

Francesco Cocco

Active aging in the model of *viviendas dotacionales*

The increase in life expectancy in western countries is bringing about significant changes in the social structure of major European cities.
In recent years the city of Barcelona has similarly experienced a change in the age structure of its residents: the trend being a general aging of the population due to a decrease in the younger generations (less than 16 years of age) combined with the constant growth of the older generations (more than 65 years of age). It is important to note that more than half of the latter is represented by women and that, when considering the octogenarian, the ratio is two out of three. Therefore, over the past few years the Catalan capital has seen a rise in single-member households, consisting mainly of elderly widowed women.
To address the housing emergency, the municipality of Barcelona has developed, through the Patronat Municipal de l'Habitatge di Barcellona (PMHB)[1], an interesting project of diversifying the housing market by offering homes designed specifically for the needs of the elderly called *viviendas dotacionales*.
These social housing units, which are regulated by the law 18/2007 concerning housing rights, are similar to those that are provided support and assistance by the local social services in Barcelona.
The *vivienda dotacional* model offers the elderly a social accommodation which is comfortable, adapted to their needs and is integrated in the local community. Moreover, such households have both direct assistance thanks to the personnel of the center, and indirect assistance through a helpline service, in order to maintain a high degree of personal autonomy for as long as possible.

---

1. The Patronat Municipal de l'Habitatge (PMHB) is one of the most representative institutions in the municipality of Barcelona. It was founded in 1927 with the purpose of building social households for people under vulnerable housing conditions. Since 2017 the PMHB has been reorganized and included in the new Institut Municipal de l'Habitatge i Rehabilitació de Barcelona (IMHAB) which performs the same functions and comprises the institution called Barcelona Gestió Urbanística SA (BAGURSA) as well.

Reina Amalia

In order to reinforce the offer of public housing and as a way to counter a shortage of building plots for social housing purposes, the municipality of Barcelona allows the construction of these structures in areas intended for services. As a result, a "hybrid" model of social housing has been created, where district services centers meet 40sq.m accommodations and other communal spaces providing amenities that can be shared with inhabitants of the same building complex. These buildings include communal spaces designed to be a natural extension of private housing spaces, capable of providing a balanced mix of services and activities, which are vital to its residents reaching their full potential.

According to the World Health Organization (WHO), a person's health, in combination with assistance services and appropriate housing represent the essential conditions for active aging.[2]

Every unit features a high versatility of the spaces and a simple pattern of distribution: an inner space which links the kitchen to the living room and the entrance, creating an open common area; and a separate sleeping area containing a double room and a fully accessible bathroom.

All apartments are barrier-free and feature all the necessary comforts allowing the elderly to live autonomously and in total safety: curbless showers, anti-slip flooring, electrical sockets accessible at a minimum height of 50cm from the floor, potable solar-powered water heating, heating, emergency lighting and alarm systems directly connected to the concierge service. In communal areas the residents can access a range of public amenities which are generally provided in the housing units: common rooms, laundries, permanent assistance service areas, libraries, cafeterias, medical practices and fitness areas. These facilities guarantee the social integration amongst residents in the housing complex and help facilitate their daily life activities. All services provided by *viviendas dotacionales* are managed directly by the social services of the municipality which handle the cleaning and maintenance of the housing units, as well as the coordination of leisure activities. The homes for the elderly are located both in historical districts and newly expanding areas of the city. To date, 1700 accommodations for the elderly have

---

2. The WHO has created a policy framework, called Active Ageing, intended to create and support the conditions for an "active ageing" to be started before reaching old age. Active ageing is based on three pillars: "Health, participation and safety for the elderly". The purpose is to shift from policies based on the needs of the elderly, regarded as passive stakeholders, to policies which recognize the right and the duty of every person to play an active role and participate in social life in every stage of life, old-age included.

been created in the 10 city districts and these services are expected to be present in those districts where they are missing or lacking.

Located in the heart of the historic centre of Barcelona, the residential building of Carrer Colomines, together with the recovery of the old market of Santa Caterina, is part of the urban regeneration of the entire Avenida Cambó area. The 59 housing units for the elderly create a curved space and the difference in height produced by the waved roofing of the opposite market, creates a fluid public space. These small public spaces featuring a strong urban feeling enrich the entrances to the market yet correspond well to the historical residences, creating small squares which then lead to the residential complex entrance. This creates the sensation of an urban market which is full of life and daily activities. The centrality of the building guarantees the proximity to public services, green areas, transportation and those activities which allow the elderly to live their lives independently, by granting access to all the necessary services within a range of 500 meters.[3]

A residential complex of 127 apartments with social tenancies is located in the district of Raval, one of the oldest in town, with 97 housing units for the elderly. The building has a huge social significance for the whole area as the ground floor hosts a day senior center and a civic center which encourage social cohesion in a multiethnic district which is lacking aggregation areas.

The architecture of the building has a vital role as uniting the district of Raval and the bordering district of Sant Antoni. So the large openings that are presented on the main façade create an architectural scenery that overlooks the square. In 2011, in the northern outskirts of Barcelona a residential complex was built within one of the access points of the urban park of Nou Barris, in order to grant the residents direct contact with nature both physically and visually.

The building, consisting of 50 apartments, community rooms, a laundry and a youth recreation area on the ground floor, is divided into three blocks and takes full advantage of the uniqueness of the area: all accommodations have the best views of the park. The circulating passages are well placed within the irregular layout of the building by expanding to create common areas and balconies on the northern and southern façades. Consequently, also the circulating space becomes a social element which decreases, together with the community spaces, the feeling of segregated individual households.

---

3. According to the World Health Organization, the elderly must walk up to a maximum of 500 meters or 15 minutes in order to easily reach a service of interest.

In close proximity to the carrer Urritia building, there are the households in Can Travi which consist of 85 apartments with social tenancies, community spaces, a civic center for the district, a leisure room and a library. The residential complex of Can Travi is located in the district of Horta-Guinardò, a suburb of the city which is undergoing an important process of redevelopment.

The project cleverly makes use of its surroundings. The spaces used to move throughout the complex such as the pathways leading to the apartments, stairwells and lifts are located in the northern part of the two areas which comprise the building, while the apartments and the social areas are located in the southern part which is surrounded by nature. This scenic atmosphere is further enhanced by a calming view of the sea. A standard accommodation, with an area of 42 sq.m consisting of a bedroom, living room, kitchen and bathroom, features internal partitions which create the sensation of large open spaces. In choosing to position the terrace within the walls of the building so as to not protrude externally, the feeling of a striking spacious area is further amplified as this shift from the bedroom to the living room makes the terrace appear as an extension of the living room. As a result, the elderly have an open "hybrid" area available, which is protected from the excessive summer heat and from where excellent views of the sea can be enjoyed.

Having such a wide open space from the terrace allows the resident to identify their own accommodation, which becomes a key element for the elderly, as it strengthens the feeling of being part of a community.

The project in Can Travi has been designed to get the most of energy saving, through a solar energy capture system created to satisfy 70% of the demand in sanitary water heating. Moreover, a centralized heating and hot sanitary water system capable of saving 35% of energy consumption has been adopted, which represents a viable alternative in this type of housing where individual gas systems are not recommended. The distribution of energy to the single apartments can be monitored individually thanks to a remote management system, which reads the meters and gives a detailed reporting of the energy consumption in each residence. In addition, the energy equipment of each household is accessible directly from the community corridor in order to offer easy access for maintenance and energy readings from the outside.

In the northern part of the city, the first apartment complex for the elderly has already been inaugurated. The 14 floors which comprise the complex have 6 apartments each. Each apartment is 42 sq.m and consists of a bedroom, living

Navas de Tolosa

room-kitchen and bathroom with all the necessary amenities to live a life in complete autonomy. In fact, the bathrooms are equipped with curbless showers as well as a centralized alarm system in both the bathroom and the bedroom. The kitchen features an electric stove and electric sockets which are accessible at a minimum height of 50 cm from the floor.

Furthermore, the residential complex features a concierge and a remote assistance system, various multifunctional rooms, multiple laundries located throughout the building and a communal outdoor space where residents can enjoy a covered lawn characterized by an innovative and lively spatial configuration.

The *vivienda dotacional* effectively addresses the needs of the elderly as it allows them to live comfortably in a place that provides all the necessary facilities which are located entirely within the complex. In addition this project is cost-effective for the residents for there are considerable savings regarding the social and health assistance services offered.

The contemporary residence is expected to adapt to social changes, to feature architectural quality, to willingly experiment with technology, care for the surrounding environment as well as to build a community. Therefore, granting the elderly housing which satisfies these criteria is vital to strengthening the traditional identity of our urban centers.

Glories

1

REINA AMALIA
Eduard Bru i Buster, Neus la Comba Mongé,
Victor Setoian Perego

2

SANTA CATERINA
EMBT Arquitectes Associats

3

CIBELES
EXE Arquitectura

4

TORRE JULIA
Paul Vidal, Sergi Pons, Ricard Galiana

5

CAN TRAVI
Sergi Serrat

6

PASSEIG URRUTIA
Joan Callís, Pia Wortham

7

NAVAS DE TOLOSA
Nogué Onzain López Arquitectes

8

RODALIES
Conxita Balcells associats

9

GLORIES
Esteve Bonell, Josep M. Gil, Marta Peris, José Toral

10

CAMÍ ANTIC DE VALENCIA
Sara Bartomeus, Anna Renau

1

REINA AMALIA
Eduard Bru i Buster, Neus la Comba Mongé, Victor Setoian Perego

The Reina Amalia residential complex in the district of Raval, in the heart of *Ciutat Vella*, revives one of the most important squares in the old town of Barcelona: Folch i Torres square.

The urban design of the building occupying three quarters of the block is U-shaped. The main façade overlooking the square shows its entire section and, merging in with the surrounding buildings, creates a single front. Therefore, the large openings that are presented on the main façade create a new architectural scenery that overlooks the square, acting as a new gateway to the district.

The floor plan features a central corridor with entrance to the accommodations located on both sides. The usual plan presents some variations on the corners, with specific architectural solutions in terms of formal distribution.

The building has a huge social significance for the entire area as the ground floor hosts a senior day center and a civic center which encourage social cohesion in a multiethnic district which is lacking aggregation areas.

Sponsoring institution
Patronat Municipal de l'Habitatge de Barcelona, PMHB

Type
Surface rights + *Viviendas dotacionales* for the elderly

Program
96 apartments for the elderly with services + 31 social housing units + 5 commercial premises + underground parking

Architects
Eduard Bru i Buster, Neus la Comba Mongé, Victor Setoian Perego

Place
Carrer de la Reina Amalia 31-33, Barcelona

Built surface
16,613 m²

Year
2011

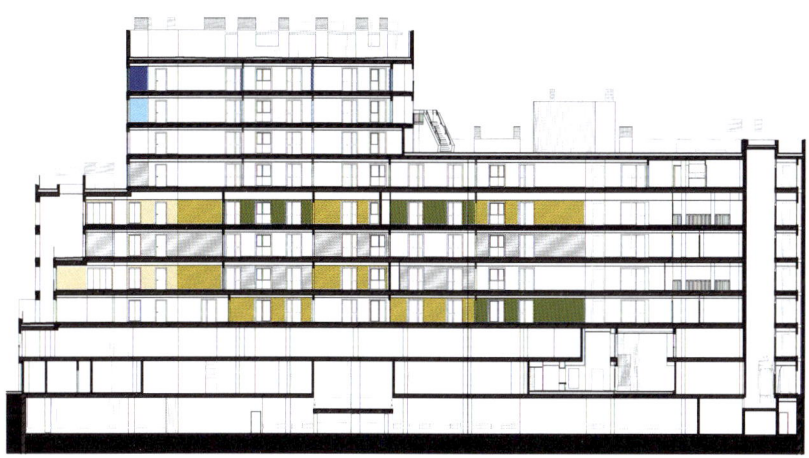

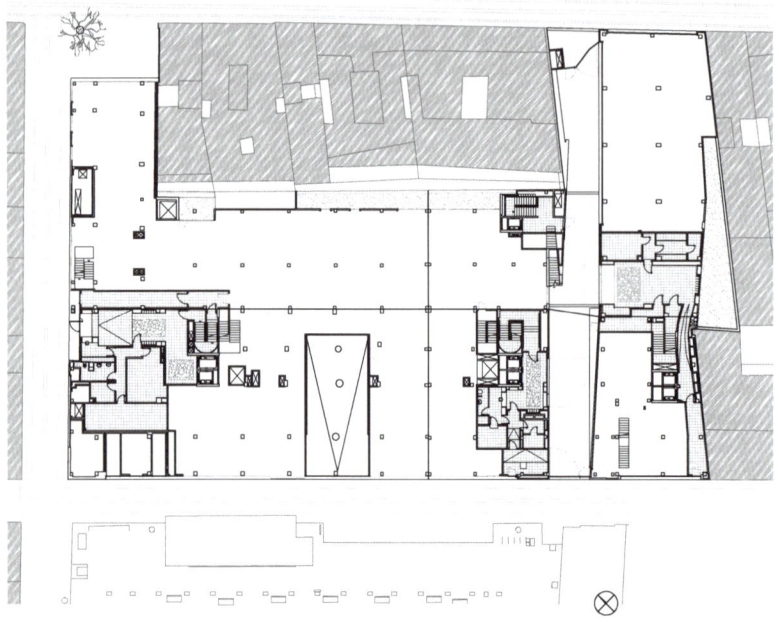

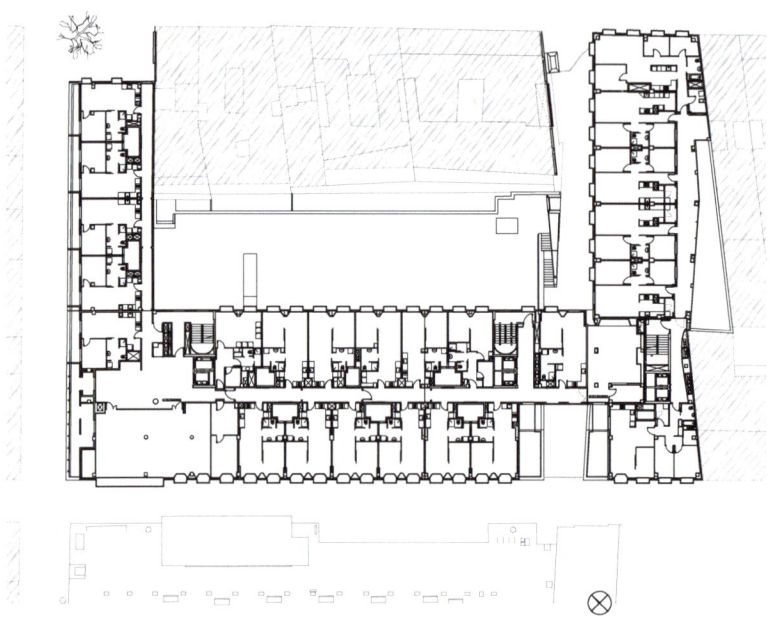

2

SANTA CATERINA
EMBT Arquitectes Associats

The residences with services for those over the age of 65, designed by Enric Miralles and Benedetta Tagliabue, are part of the regeneration program of the entire area of Avenida Cambó, together with the intervention in the old market of Santa Caterina, which is a highly degraded section of the old town. The residential building generates a curved space, and the difference in height produced by the waved roofing of the opposite market creates a fluid public space.

The relationship between the building and the market is necessary in order to understand this architectural work. The two spaces merge together in some points, creating small public spaces with a strong urban feeling which enrich the entrances to the market and correspond well to the historical residences.

The centrality of the building guarantees the proximity to public services, green areas, transportation and those activities which allow the elderly to live their lives independently.

The project features a standard housing model consisting of a living room, kitchen, double bedroom and bathroom. In addition to this, there are communal rooms and nursing services to assist the users.

Sponsoring institution
Patronat Municipal de l'Habitatge de Barcelona, PMHB

Type
Viviendas dotacionales for the elderly

Program
59 apartments for the elderly with services

Architects
EMBT Arquitectes Associats (Enric Miralles, Benedetta Tagliabue)

Place
Carrer Colomines 1-5, Barcelona

Built surface
16,251 m²

Year
2004

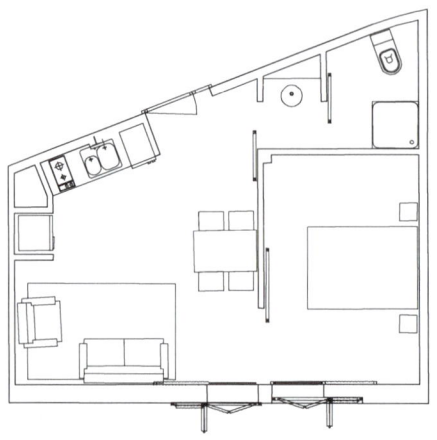

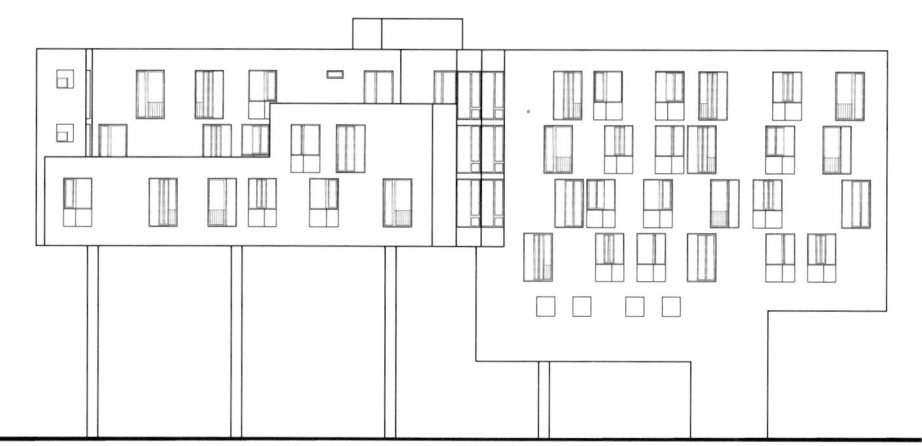
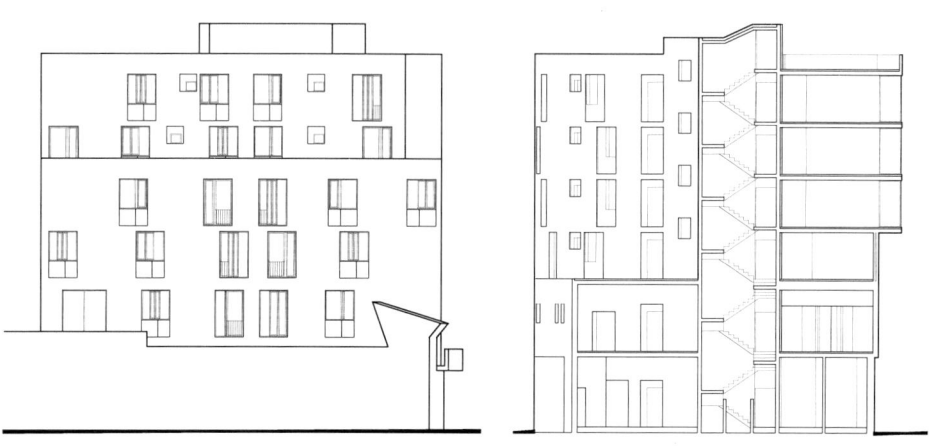

CIBELES
EXE Arquitectura

The building is located in the district of Gracia, in the plot which was previously occupied by the historic Cibeles dancehall.
The building consists of two different parts with separated gateways: the first three floors and the basement are designed for the activities of the Primary healthcare center (CAP). Instead, the following four floors feature 32 apartments for the elderly.
The Cibeles *vivienda dotacional* is one of the four experimental buildings by the European investigating project on the High-Combi system, which captures solar energy to satisfy 60% of the demand in energy consumption (hot sanitary water, heating and cooling). The building has obtained an "A" energy certification, becoming the second building in Barcelona reaching the maximum energy qualification according to the Catalan Institution of Energy (ICAEN).
For this reason, the project received the Premio Endesa prize for the most sustainable residential building in 2011.

Sponsoring institution
Patronat Municipal de l'Habitatge de Barcelona, PMHB

Type
Viviendas dotacionales for the elderly

Program
32 appartments for the elderly with services + Primary healthcare center

Architects
EXE Arquitectura (Jaume Valor, Marc Obrador)

Place
Carrer Corsega 363, Barcelona

Built Surface
5,880 m²

Year
2011

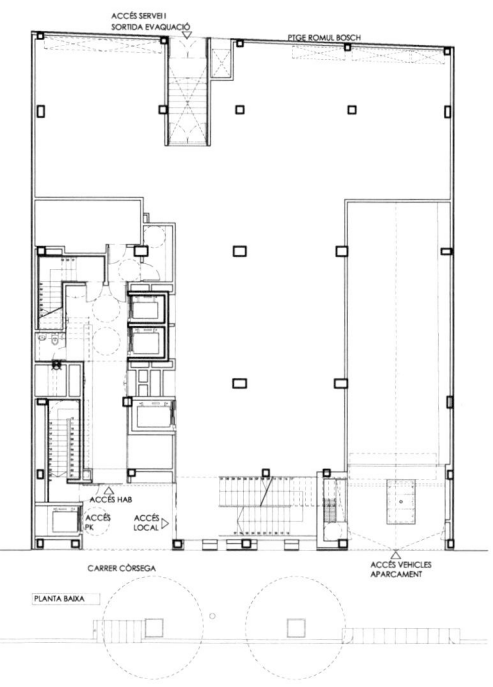
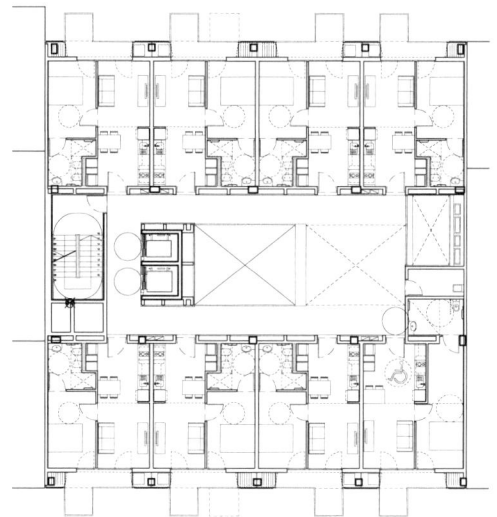

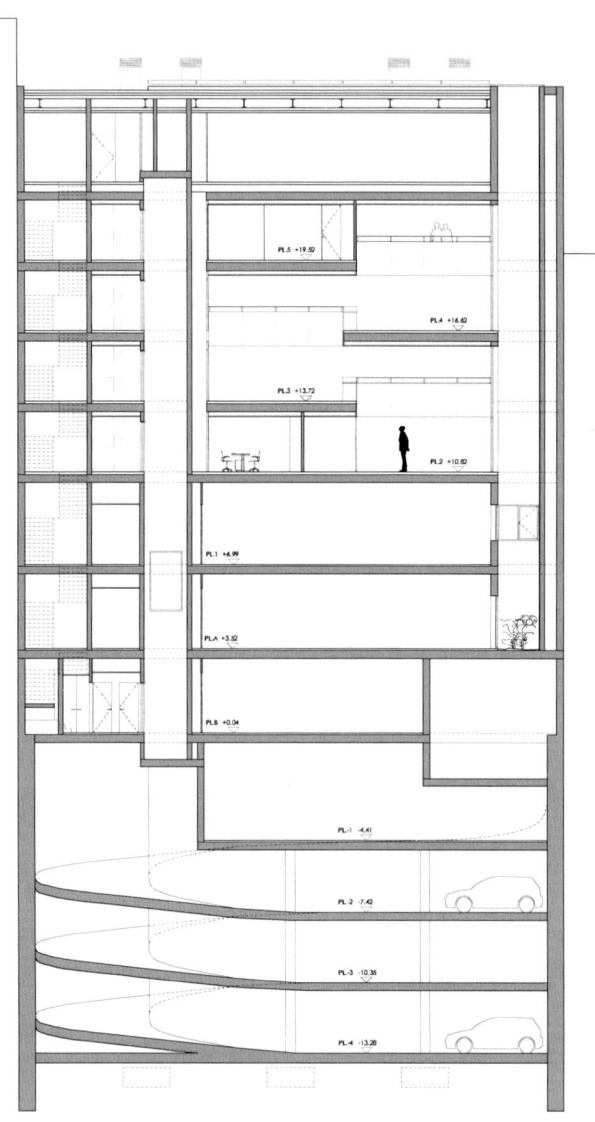

4

TORRE JULIA
Paul Vidal, Sergi Pons, Ricard Galiana

Torre Julia, designed for the independent elderly, has quickly become one of the symbols of postolympic Barcelona.

The 17 floor tower, which won the Barcelona city prize for architecture and town-planning, is divided in three parts. Each part features a communal space where the shared activities organized by the residents take place. These spaces represent the core of the project and are clearly highlighted in the façade. The tower presents large corridors with views of the city, external stairs, double height spaces and a terrace with a garden enabling the elderly to socialize and live their lives independently.

Sponsoring institution
Patronat Municipal de l'Habitatge de Barcelona, PMHB

Type
Viviendas dotacionales for the elderly

Program
77 apartments for the elderly with services + underground parking

Architects
Paul Vidal, Sergi Pons, Ricard Galiana

Place
Via Favencia 348, Barcelona

Built surface
8,391 m²

Year
2011

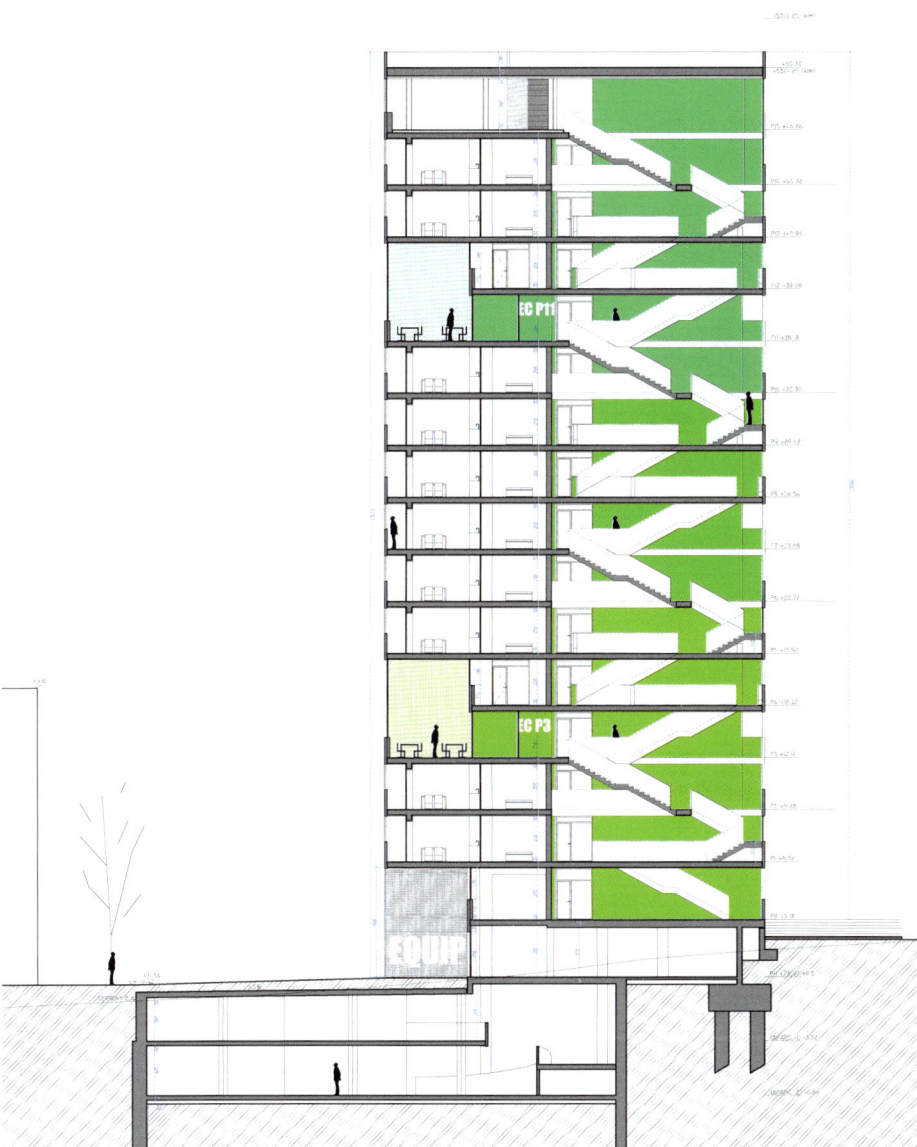

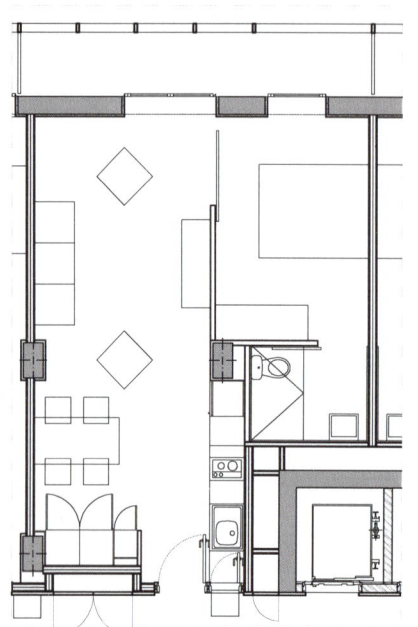
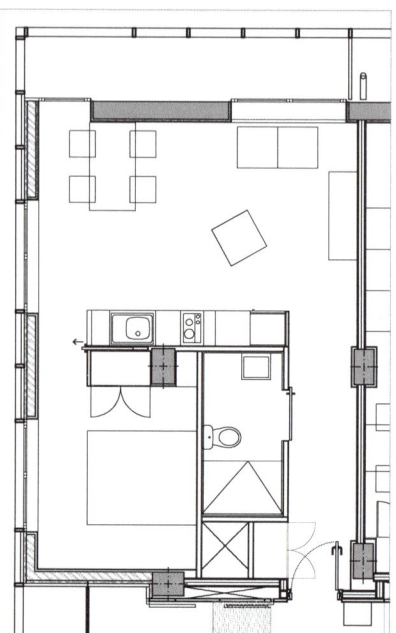

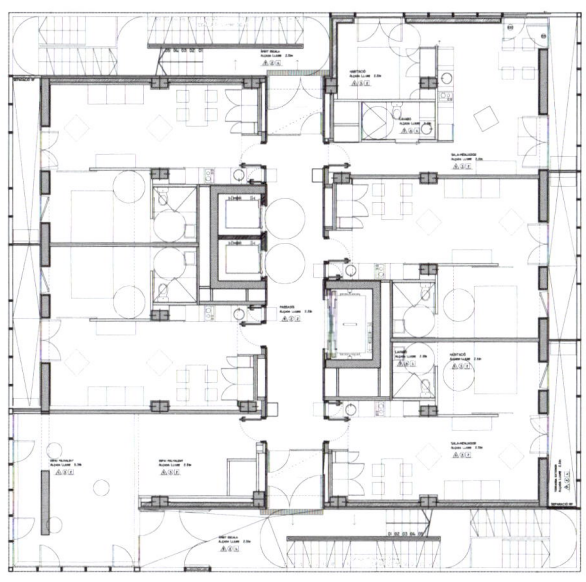

5

CAN TRAVI
Sergi Serrat Guillen, Ginés Egea, Cristina García

The building, located in the northern suburb of Barcelona, consists of 85 apartments with social tenancies and assistant services, in addition to several halls hosting activities designed for the neighbors of the district. The project cleverly makes use of its surroundings. The areas intended for services (corridors, maintenance closets, bathrooms, kitchens and dressing room) are located in the northern part of the two rows of apartments which comprise the building, while the social areas are located in the southern part which is surrounded by nature. The standard accommodation, consisting of a bedroom, living room, kitchen and bathroom, features internal partitions which create the sensation of larger open spaces. The choice to position the terrace within the walls of the building so as to not protrude externally results in a shift from the bedroom to the living room, making the terrace appear as an extension of the living room. As a result, the elderly have an open "hybrid" area available, which is protected from the excessive summer heat and from where excellent views of the sea can be enjoyed.

Sponsoring institution
Patronat Municipal de l'Habitatge de Barcelona, PMHB

Type
Viviendas dotacionales for the elderly

Program
85 apartments for the elderly with services + civic center + leisure room + underground parking

Architects
Sergi Serrat Guillen, Ginés Egea, Cristina García

Place
Can Travi 30, Barcellona

Built surface
9,345 m²

Year
2011

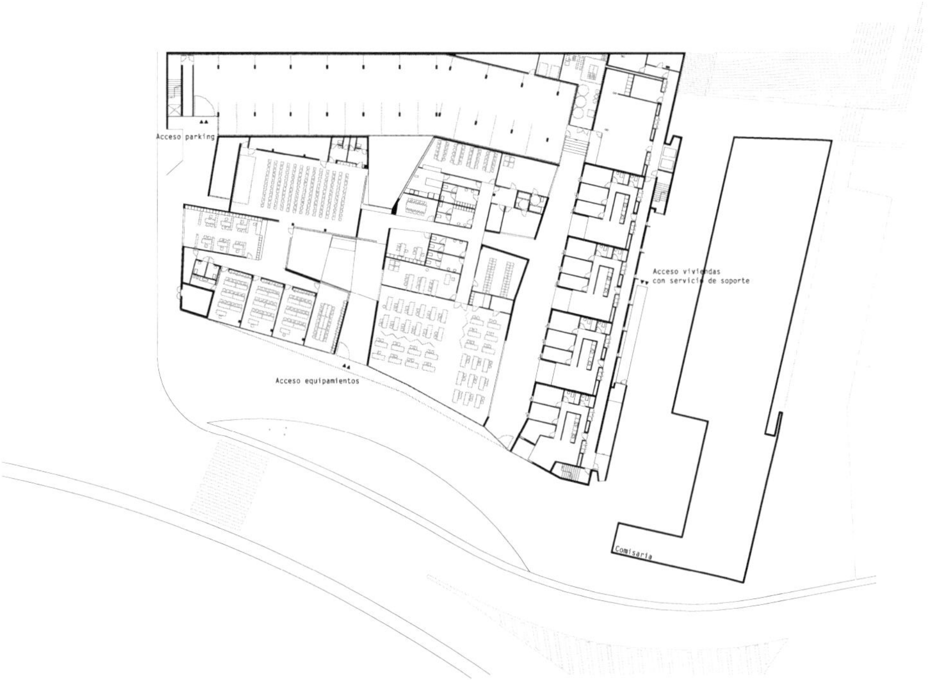
Acceso parking
Acceso viviendas
con servicio de soporte
Acceso equipamientos
Comisaria

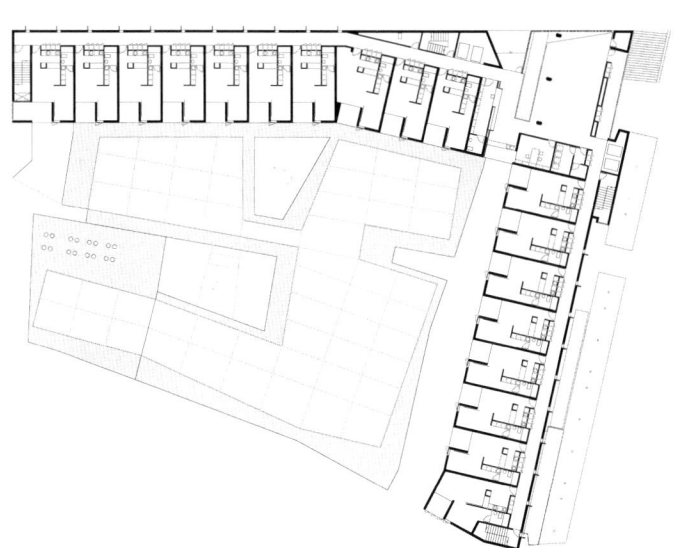

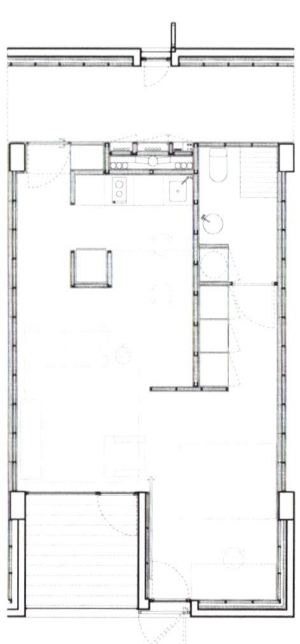

76 Social Housing Barcelona

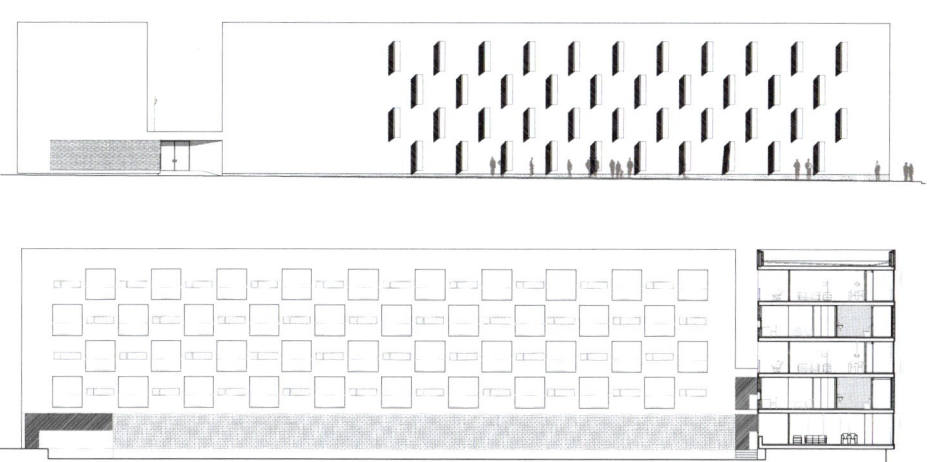

6

PASSEIG URRUTIA
Joan Callís, Pia Wortham

Located in the northern suburbs of Barcelona, on the border of the Nou Barris urban park, this residential complex for the elderly is built taking into considering the rolling terrain and therefore as a consequence, grants the residents direct contact with nature both physically and visually, thanks to an attentive orientation of the openings of the households towards the green areas and the big lake. The shape of the building is consistent with the one of the existing historical building that is irregular and uneven. Such an architectural consistency between new and existing works is due to the necessity to create an open court for the residents. The distribution corridor inside the building maintains this irregular shape, by opening, closing and following the dimension of the building, eventually leading into balconies and gathering spaces between the northern and the southern façades. This way the distribution space becomes a key element in connecting the complex. Every housing unit, oriented in order to guarantee the best views of the park, has a surface of 45 m2 and consists of a kitchen integrated with a living room, a bedroom and a bathroom, flanked by two multifunctional halls and a communal laundry.

Sponsoring institution
Patronat Municipal de l'Habitatge de Barcelona, PMHB

Type
Viviendas dotacionales for the elderly

Program
50 apartments for the elderly with services

Architects
Joan Callís, Pia Wortham

Place
Passeig Urrutia 5, Barcelona

Built surface
3,500 m²

Year
2008

PASEIG D'URRUTIA
CARRER DE FABRA I PUIG
SALA POLIVALENT 1
SALA POLIVALENT 2

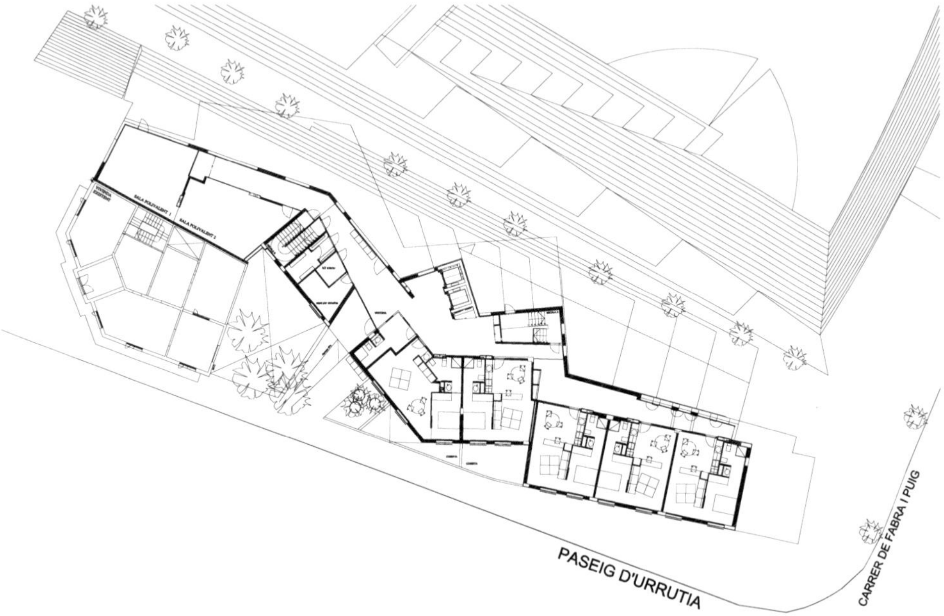

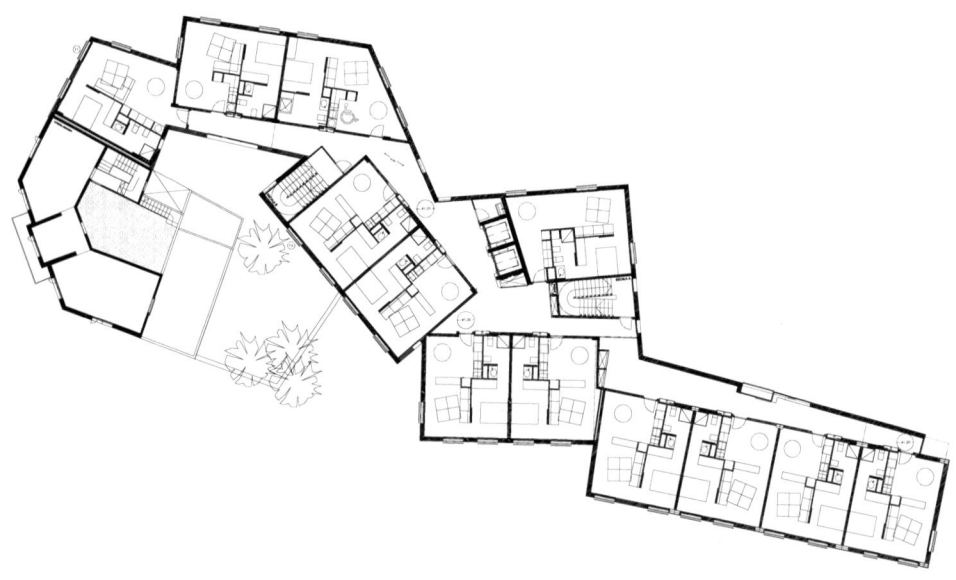

FAÇANA PASSEIG
URRUTIA

7

NAVAS DE TOLOSA
Nogué Onzain López Arquitectes

The Navas de Tolosa building is organized in two separated blocks which overlook a symbolic point of the district: a corner formed by two main roads. The typical Eixample block by Ildefons Cerdà, with the corner solution (*chaflán*), is dematerialized creating a viewing cone of the internal square surrounded by a building of six floors. The first housing block hosts 78 apartments for the younger generations and a preschool on the ground floor. The second block hosts 76 households for the elderly and a civic center on the ground and the first floor. The choice to renounce the natural transversal ventilation of the households (through mechanical means) in order to have a good balance between the length of the façade (7m) and the depth of the household (6m) results in a good relationship with the outside. The elements of the household are designed to increase the perception of the space: the corridor transforms into a dressing rooms leading to the bathroom where there is a generous space for the washing machine. The small terrace includes a drying rack which becomes part of the formal aspect of the façade. The huge sliding door linking the room and the hall allows for a higher dimensional perception. Social activities for the elderly take place in the two communal halls on the ground floor, on the large terrace on the third floor and in the cozy urban garden in the loft.

Sponsoring institution
Patronat Municipal de l'Habitatge de Barcelona, PMHB

Type
Surface rights + *Viviendas dotacionales* for the elderly

Program
76 apartments for the elderly with services + 46 social housing apartments + preschool + civic center + underground parking

Architects
Nogué Onzain López Arquitectes

Place
Carrer Navas de Tolosa 312, Barcelona

Built surface
18,722 m²

Year
2012

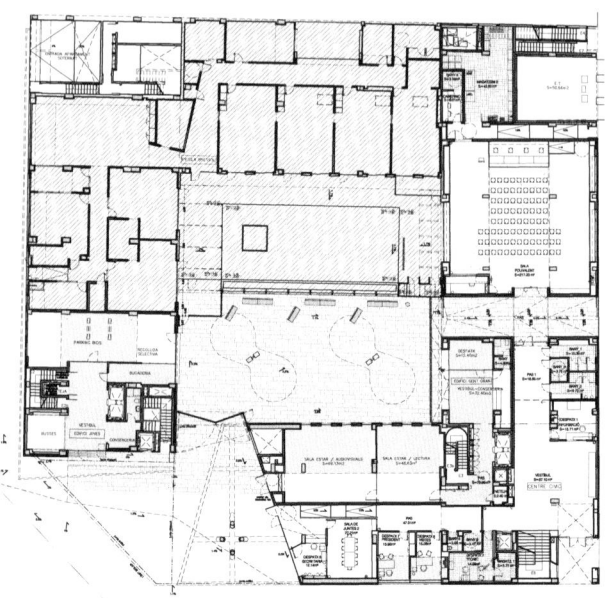

8

RODALIES
Conxita Balcells associats

The Rodalies project presents such a significant space articulated around a big central patio. The northern, southern and eastern façades follow the perimeter of the block, while the western façade curves adapting to the urban feel of the opposite historical district of Barceloneta. The accommodations feature a clear separation between the living and sleeping area. In each apartment the kitchen and the bathroom run parallel to the accessing corridor in order to allow an easy and secure inspection of the equipment from outside the apartment. Moreover, the apartments run perpendicular to the façade granting a natural ventilation and illumination of the façade. Each apartment is designed to have natural ventilation throughout the household.

Sponsoring institution
Patronat Municipal de l'Habitatge de Barcelona, PMHB

Type
Surface rights

Program
128 apartments with Surface Rights

Architects
Conxita Balcells associats

Place
Carrer Doctor Aiguader 21, Barcelona

Built surface
14,236 m²

Year
2014

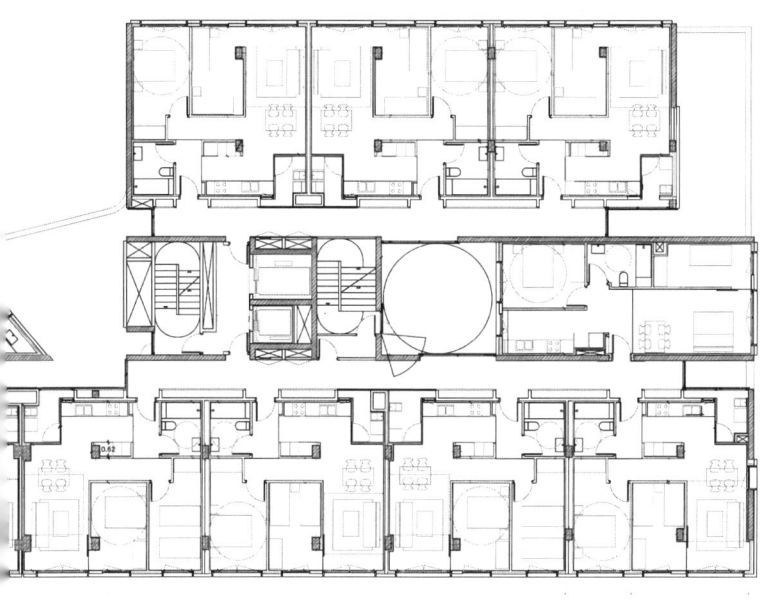

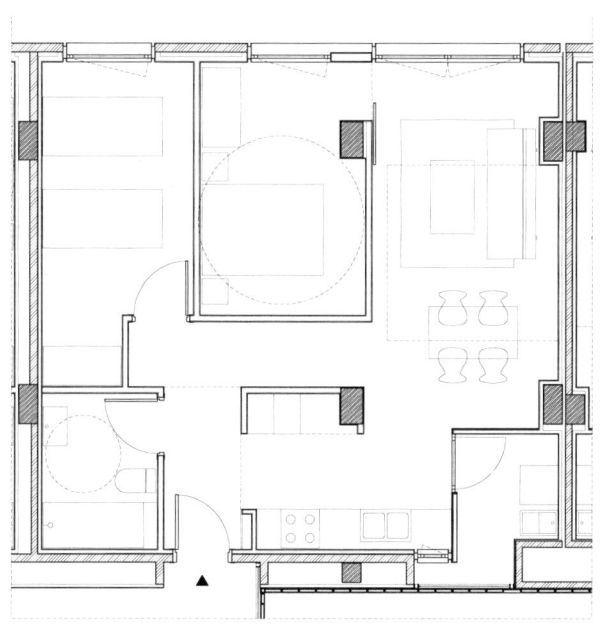
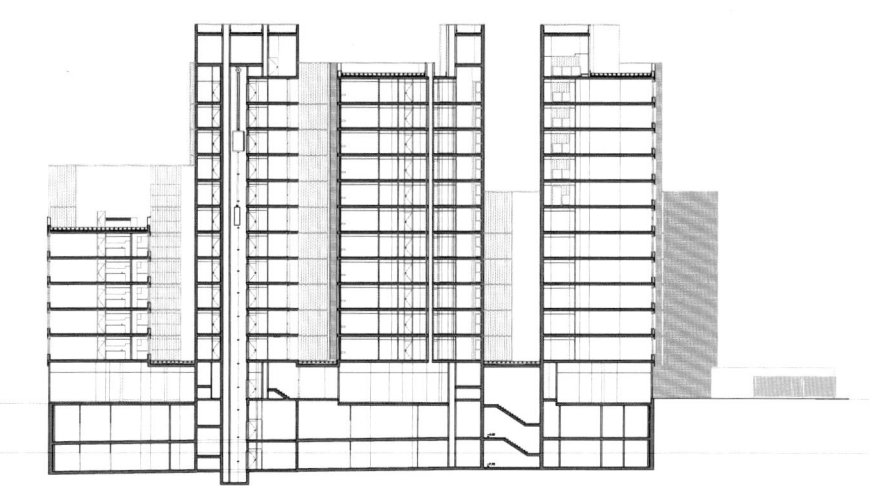

GLORIES
Esteve Bonell, Josep Maria Gil, Marta Peris, Jose Manuel Toral

The *vivienda dotacional* with services for the elderly of Glories is part of a housing program promoted by the municipality of Barcelona which includes the construction of 225 apartments with social tenancy and surface rights for people under vulnerable housing conditions. The building consists of a ground floor with public spaces (mental health center, primary healthcare (CAP) and a civic center for the district) and three buildings for housing purposes, where the apartments for the elderly and shared spaces are located. Each building features a maximum of eight apartments, distributed throughout the different floors through a central corridor that changes its section at the end, and expands in order to give access to a big communal terrace linking the three buildings on the first floor. In the upper terrace of each building there is a space for communal laundry and a place to hang dry the wash, a solarium and an area for an urban vegetable garden for the elderly. Private spaces consist of 40 m2 apartments displayed around a central core where the bathroom is located. This solution allows the residents to move, thanks to the sliding doors inside each apartment, in a circular way without barriers around the accommodation, making maximum use of the available space. This complex has been selected among the 40 most interesting works of the year 2017 according to the international architectural prize of the Mies Van der Rohe Foundation.

Sponsoring institution
Patronat Municipal de l'Habitatge de Barcelona, PMHB

Type
Viviendas dotacionales for the elderly

Program
105 apartments for the elderly + mental health center + primary healthcare center (CAP) + civic center for the district

Architects
Esteve Bonell, Josep Maria Gil, Marta Peris, Jose Manuel Toral

Place
Carrer Bolivia 45-47-49, Barcelona

Built surface
27,400 m²

Year
2017

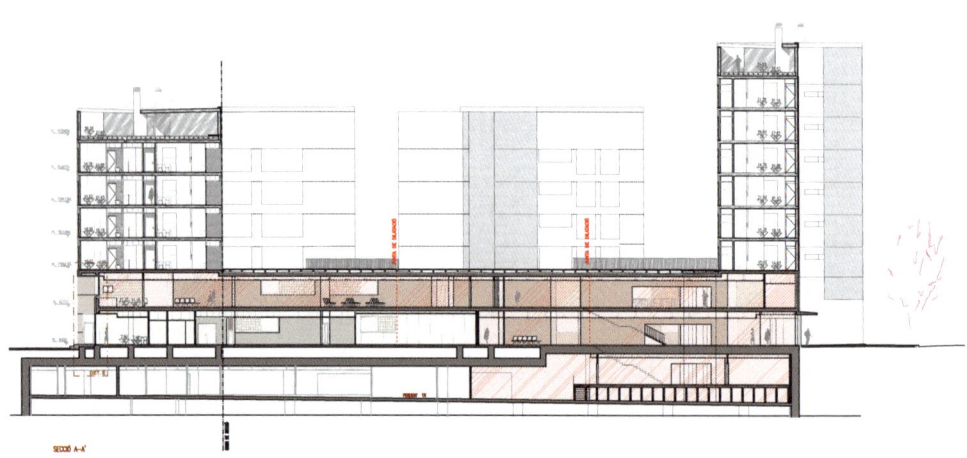

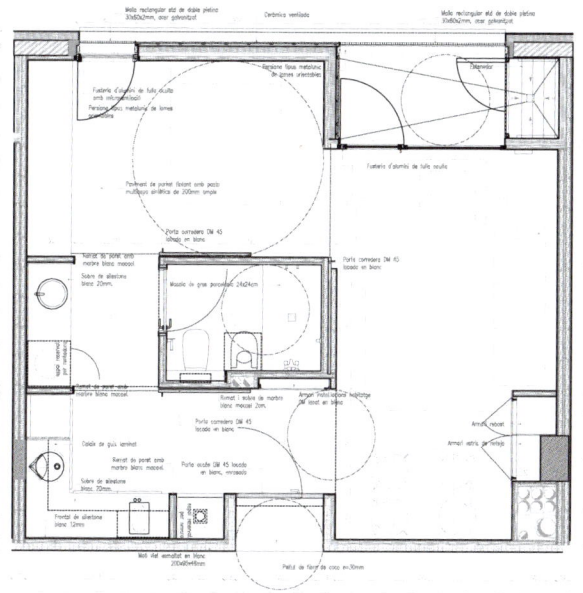

10

CAMÍ ANTIC DE VALENCIA
Sara Bartomeus, Anna Renau

The complex consists of five buildings of various heights (between 2 and 8 floors) connecting to each other through a series of walkways and communal spaces, recalling the complex shape of the industrial spaces of Poblenou. The inner patio is essential to the project as it establishes a relationship with the households and, on a larger scale, with the surrounding open spaces, and thus creates two different landscapes. One of these patios has a more urban feeling and is delimited on the ground floor by the civic center overlooked by the accommodations for young people, while the other patio, accessible from the road and the surrounding public space, is an urban vegetable garden for the elderly. The complex closes off from the road with a façade featuring small openings and opens towards the inner court thanks to a more complex glass façade, with different layers that guarantee both the architectural unity of the housing complex and the differentiation of the different households, buildings and orientations.

Sponsoring institution
Patronat Municipal de l'Habitatge de Barcelona, PMHB

Type
Surface rights + *Viviendas dotacionales* for the elderly

Program
88 apartments for the Young + 76 apartments for the elderly + communal spaces + civic center + underground parking

Architects
Sara Bartomeus, Anna Renau

Place
Carrer Camí Antic de Valencia 96, Barcelona

Built Surface
10,000 m²

Year
2009

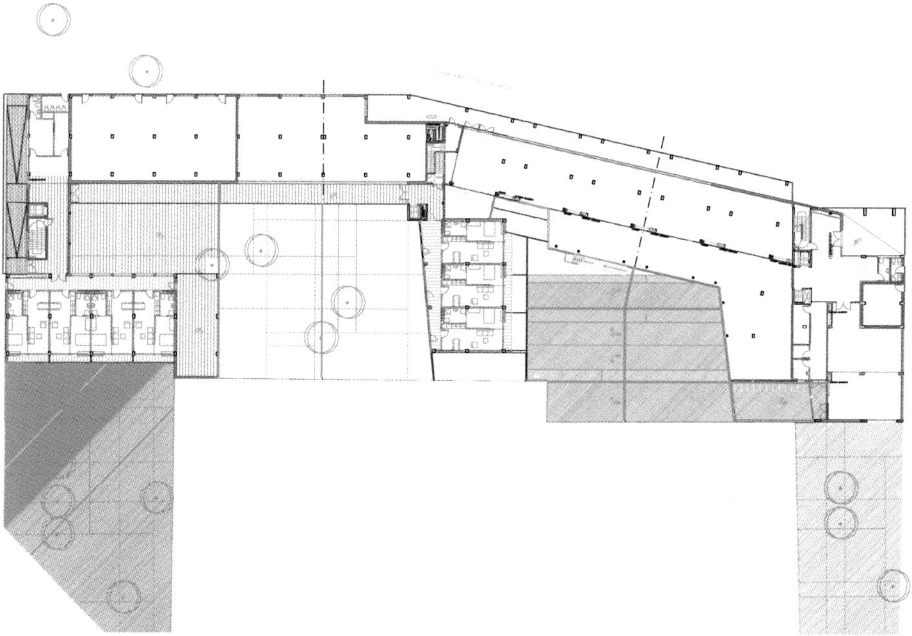

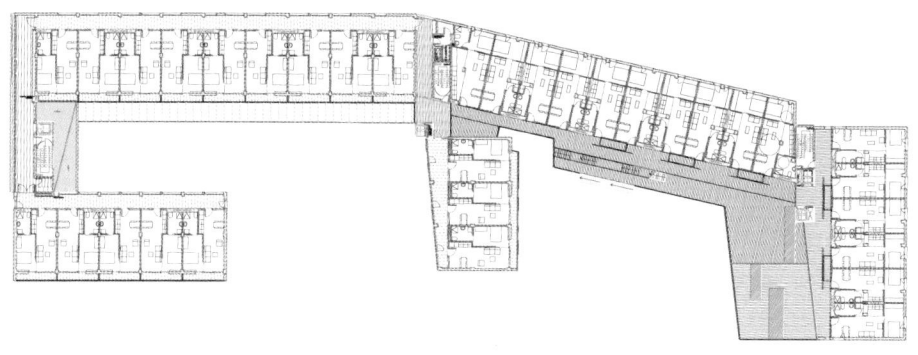

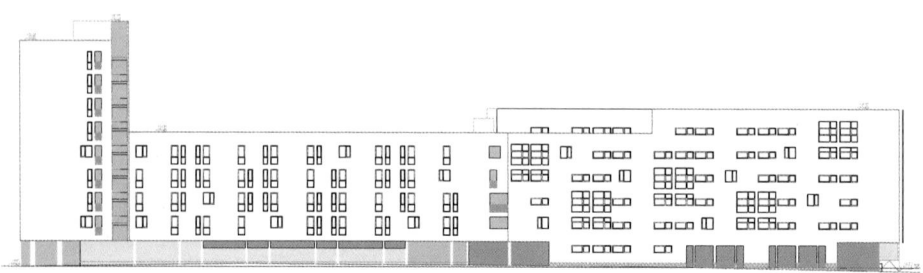

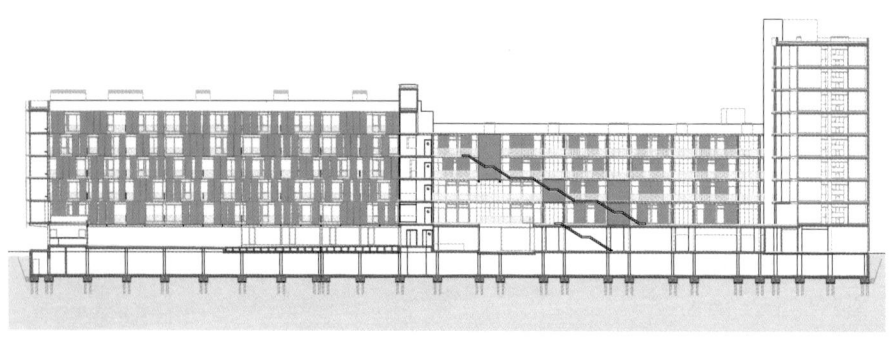

Josep Mª Montaner

Public housing: the Barcelona model

It can be stated that there is a conventional "Barcelona model" in the public housing policy of the city, with its qualities and defects. Over the last decade, public housing initiatives have promoted small and medium-sized operations, which seldom exceed a hundred housing units. The most recent operations were designed within areas allowing the creation of a maximum of 20 or 30 households.

Among the different projects planned by the municipality of Barcelona, the social housing initiatives for the elderly stand out. In addition to this, there are about twenty existing buildings, totaling 1,200 households with communal services. These projects realized by the old "Patronat Municipal de l'Habitatge", today known as "Institut Municipal de l'Habitatge i Rehabilitació" (IMHAB), represent a solution deeply appreciated both by the inhabitants and the international community. Living in these buildings allows the residents to have their own house and, at the same time, to enjoy services, communal spaces, have company and join in an activity if they want or need it.

These initiatives are well-designed within their context contributing to its improvement. These buildings integrate well in the urban scheme by recreating it, as seen for instance in the households in calle Reina Amalia, within the Ciutat Vella, by Eduard Bru, Neus Lacomba and Victor Setoian. Other households are located in more defined urban schemes, as the Eixample district (the social households of the old "Cibeles", by Exe Arquitectura, or the residential complex with services in calle Navas de Tolosa by Nogué Onzain López Arquitectures SL). Furthermore, there are operations creating the city where different realities and levels of urban archeology coexisted, as for the Rodalies complex (which will host the new IMHAB offices and services on the ground floor) by Conxita Balcells Associats. In addition to this, other projects build a new area of centrality and meeting area as is in the case of the social households in the Santa Caterina market in calle Coromines by Enric Miralles/Benedetta Tagliabue (EMTB Arquitectes Associats), where the project relates to and recovers sections of the medieval city.

Over the last few years, due to town planning changes, an increasing number of buildings have been converted to public housing units, resulting in an improvement of the urban quality and in a saving, in terms of investments, considering the scale of the operations and the reutilization of an existing structure of the buildings as a basis for the new services. This is the case of the famous initiative in calle Bolivia, behind Plaza de Glories, by Josep Maria

Gil, Marta Peris and José Manuel Toral, which is also presented in this space. The complex consists of 105 households, with services on the ground floor, and a green area surrounding the three buildings, which include communal services on the different floors. The external finish is made of white light concrete, and each household is 40m2 with a circular distribution layout around the bathroom.

The households for the young and the elderly in Poblenou, which are part of the Camí Antic de Valencia project by the architects Sara Bartomeus and Anna Renau, are a representative example. The project has an urban shape called "redent" and creates several communal and transition spaces through the usage of closed and open corridors and two big patios. It is an urban and a social experiment: the building consists of 88 households for the young and 76 households for the elderly and a free space for both residential categories. The two parts of the complex present a shape relating to the urban context of the surrounding streets, by following their orientation. The households for young couples have a surface slightly bigger than 30m2 but they all feature large external access corridors. Other residential complexes, like the Torre Julia project by Pau Vidal, Sergi Pons and Ricard Galiana or the Calle Urrutia project by Joan Callís and Pía Worthan, in the working class and symbolic district of Parque del Norte, are unique and monumental (the first one with a tower design, and the other one with a wavy form like that of a snake). Finally, there are initiatives, like the Can Travi project by Sergi Serrat, which bring quality to the suburban residential scheme.

Most of the projects were awarded after an open competition in two stages (curriculum and preliminary project) and they were designed by the most illustrious groups of the city specialized in collective and social housing. Most of these buildings are designed to be rented, while there is a decrease in the initiatives aimed at relocating inhabitants from other districts. As a matter of fact, the new "Plan por el Derecho a la Vivienda en Barcelona (2016-2025)" states that over the decade 80% of the new buildings will be for rent and only 20% will be for surface rights and other trends.

Here we have a weakness in the housing policy over the last decade. Several initiatives were meant for sale, while other projects have entered the free market over the years. Consequently, the total of public operations did not reach 1.5% in 2015, that is 6,500 households out of 30,000 units built on public plots with public funds.

Another factor to take into consideration, in addition to the positive improvement in the quality of the operations, is the lack of initiatives, averaging 10 projects under construction per year. Nowadays there are 66 public housing works under construction in Barcelona. It is a selected production, but it is completely inadequate as thousands of public households are urgently needed.

Today the focus is set on new and big challenges that still cannot be presented in this volume. Among these challenges there are the "co-vivienda" (co-housing) where the public plot is managed by cooperatives (two of these experiments have just been completed and five of them are still under construction), the enhancement of the refurbishments and acquisitions of buildings for social purposes, the increase in social households with services and the promotion of representative operations like the 250 households in Plaza de Glories, opposite the new "Parc de la Cornucopia". This project was awarded after an international competition and it will be co-managed by four groups of architects.

In addition to representing a new way of proceeding for the city of Barcelona, through the coordination of the designing activity by different groups, this monumental work, consisting of public households, represents a major step forward for a sound and sustainable housing, flexibility and gender equality.

Above all, despite the efforts made, the issue of public housing is still to be solved, and all the possible means and instruments should be used in order to improve it.

Editorial Series
Sustainable and affordable housing

Editor In Chief
Massimo Faiferri

Scientific Commitee
Enric Batlle
Gonçalo Byrne
Anne Lacaton
Joe Noero
Federico Soriano
Jean Philippe Vassal

Architecture At Alghero .Master
Sustainable
and Affordable
Housing

http://housing.aaamaster.it/

For information contact
DADU, Dipartimento di Architettura, Design e Urbanistica,
Palazzo del Pou Salit - Piazza Duomo 6, 07041 Alghero (SS).
e-mail aaamaster@uniss.it
www.architettura.uniss.it/ita/Didattica/Master

Academic board of the Master's Degree in "Sustainable and affordable housing"

Master's Director
Massimo Faiferri - Università di Sassari

Academic board of the Master's Degree
Valter Caldana, Universidade Presiteriana Mackenzie Sao Paulo
Arnaldo Cecchini- Università di Sassari
Enrico Cicalò - Università di Sassari
Josep Mias Gifrè - Università di Sassari
Alessandro Plaisant - Università di Sassari
Ignasi Perez Arnal - Visiting professor presso l'Università di Sassari
Pedro Rodrigues, Universidade Tecnica de Lisboa
Silvia Serreli - Università di Sassari
Stefan Tischer- Università di Sassari

Tutoring Teachers
Samanta Bartocci
Mauro Cossu
Filippo De Dominicis
Jacopo Galli
Fabrizio Pusceddu

Sustainable and affordable housing is an international book series founded with the aim of conveying the studies, research and cultural initiatives developed within the international Master's Degree Level 2 of the same name set up at the Department of Architecture, Design and Urbanism of the University of Sassari, in cooperation with the Facultade de Arquitectura of the Universidade Tecnica de Lisboa, the Universidade Presbiteriana of Sao Paulo and the Autonomous Region of Sardinia - Department of Labour, Vocational Training, Cooperation and Social Security.

The series uses a text evaluation system based on an anonymous peer-review by lecturers of the Publisher's Research Committee.

The creation of this series has been possible thanks to the contribution of:

With the collaboration of
Institut Municipal de l'Habitatge de Barcelona

Photo credits
Photos by ©Stefano Ferrando, with the collaboration of Carla Canetto

Acknowledgements
Ayuntamiento de Barcelona, Joaquim Pascual Sangrà, Immaculada Santos Castilla, Josep Maria Montaner, Raimondo Pibiri, Pino Frau

SOCIAL HOUSING BARCELONA

Authors
Massimo Faiferri - Francesco Cocco

Published by
LISt Lab
info@listlab.eu
listlab.eu

Whith the collaboration of
Ajuntament de Barcelona

Art Director & Production
Blacklist Creative, BCN
blacklist-creative.com

Translation Diego Di Matteo, Erika Sokach

ISBN 9788899854751

Printed and bound in the European Union
2019

**Series sustainable and affordable
                housing collection**

Prohibited total or partial reproduction
of this book by any means, without permission
of the author and publisher.

All rights reserved
© of the edition LISt Lab
© of the text the authors
© of the images the authors, all the images of the
cities are taken from URBACT Local Action Plans.

Sales, Marketing & Distribution
distribution@listlab.eu
listlab.eu/en/distribuzione/

Scientific Committee of the List editions
Eve Blau – Harvard GSD (U.S.A.), Maurizio Carta
– Università di Palermo (IT), Alfredo Ramirez –
Architectural Association London (UK), Alberto
Cecchetto – Università di Venezia (IT), Stefano De
Martino – Università di Innsbruck (AU), Corrado
Diamantini – Università di Trento (IT), Antonio De
Rossi – Università di Torino (IT), Franco Farinelli
– Università di Bologna (IT), Carlo Gasparrini –
Università di Napoli (IT), Manuel Gausa – Università di Genova (IT), Giovanni Maciocco – Università
di Sassari/Alghero (IT), Mosè Ricci – Università di
Trento (IT), Roger Riewe – Università di Graz (AU),
Pino Scaglione – Università di Trento (IT)

LIStLab is an editorial workshop, based in Europe,
that works on contemporary issues. LISt Lab not
only publishes, but also researches, proposes,
promotes, produces, creates networks.

LIStLab is a green company committed to
respect the environment. Paper, ink, glues and all
processings come from short supply chains and
aim at limiting pollution. The print run of books
and magazines is based on consumption patterns,
thus preventing waste of paper and surpluses. LISt
Lab aims at the responsibility of the authors and
markets, towards the knowledge of a new publishing culture based on resource management.